Simply JAZZ

GRADES 4–5

Arrangements for piano solo
by **Barrie Carson Turner**

FABER *ff* MUSIC

First published in 2009 by Faber Music Ltd
Bloomsbury House 74–77 Great Russell Street London WC1B 3DA
Music processed by Jeanne Roberts
Cover design by Kenosha
Printed in England by Caligraving Ltd

ISBN10: 0-571-53269-1
EAN13: 978-0-571-53269-8

Contents

CHICAGO FISHER *page 4*

MOOD INDIGO MILLS/ELLINGTON/BIGARD *page 5*

THE DARKTOWN STRUTTERS' BALL BROOKS *page 6*

LET'S DO IT (LET'S FALL IN LOVE) PORTER *page 7*

THE BARE NECESSITIES GILKYSON *page 8*

ALEXANDER'S RAGTIME BAND BERLIN *page 10*

BILL BAILEY WON'T YOU COME HOME CANNON *page 12*

YOU MAKE ME FEEL SO YOUNG GORDON/MYROW *page 14*

STORMY WEATHER KOEHLER/ARLEN *page 16*

NIGHT AND DAY PORTER *page 18*

I GOT RHYTHM GERSHWIN/GERSHWIN *page 20*

IT AIN'T NECESSARILY SO GERSHWIN/HEYWARD/HEYWARD/GERSHWIN *page 22*

THE BIRTH OF THE BLUES DE SYLVA/BROWN/HENDERSON *page 24*

Chicago

Frank Sinatra's performance of this song in the film *The Joker is Wild* is probably the best-known recording of it. The lyrics of the song recall the attractions of the city of Chicago.

Words and Music by Fred Fisher

Mood Indigo

The American pianist and band leader Duke Ellington wrote *Mood Indigo* jointly with the jazz clarinettist Barney Bigard. The 'indigo' of the title clearly refers to the rich 'blue' harmonies used.

Words by Irving Mills
Music by Duke Ellington and Barney Bigard

Slowly, with expression

The Darktown Strutters' Ball

The jazz musicians and band leaders Jimmy Dorsey and Benny Goodman have both recorded this song. A recording of the song in 1917 may have been the first commercially-made jazz record.

Words and Music by Shelton Brooks

Moderately, with a swing

Let's Do It (Let's Fall In Love)

In 1928 Cole Porter enjoyed his first Broadway hit with the musical *Paris*, which featured the song *Let's Do It, (Let's Fall In Love)*. The song lyrics cleverly portray the act of falling in love through the eyes of many different creatures.

Words and Music by Cole Porter

The Bare Necessities

This popular song appears in the Disney film *The Jungle Book*. It is performed by the bear Baloo, singing about his own view of the 'necessities of life'. Louis Armstrong also recorded this song.

Words and Music by Terry Gilkyson

Brightly

34
40
45
mf
50
55
60
f

Alexander's Ragtime Band

Alexander's Ragtime Band was the Russian-born American songwriter Irving Berlin's first major hit, written when he was only twenty-three. The composer went on to write over 1000 songs.

Words and Music by Irving Berlin

Moderate march

16
19
22
25
29

Bill Bailey Won't You Come Home

This song, dating from 1902, is in Victorian music hall style and is a popular title in the 'trad jazz' repertoire. The songwriter Hughie Cannon wrote both the music and lyrics.

Words and Music by Hughie Cannon

Moderate swing

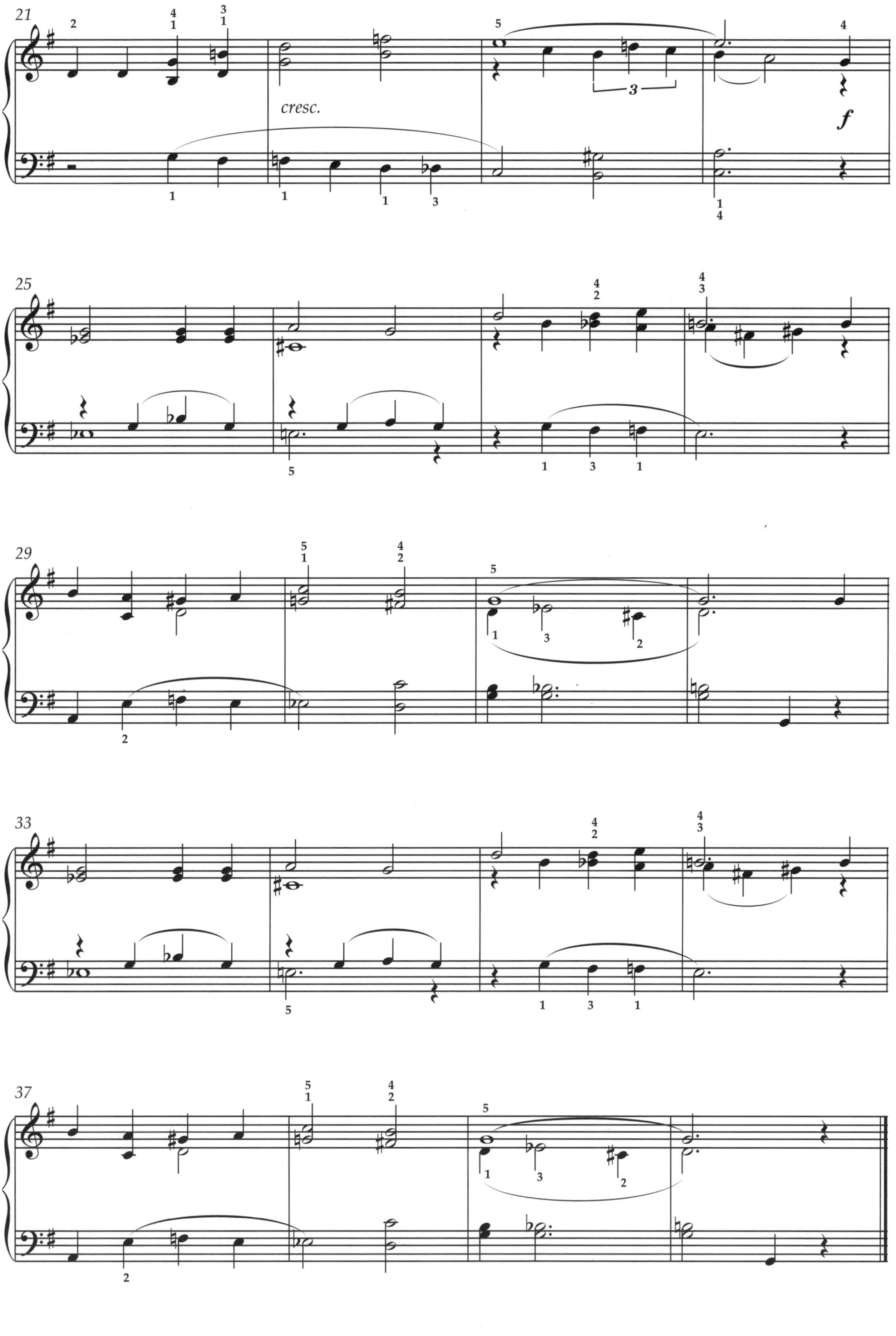
21
cresc.
f
25
29
33
37

You Make Me Feel So Young

You Make Me Feel So Young dates from 1946. Russian-born composer Josef Myrow was known mainly as a film composer, even though this song is probably his best-known work. The lyricist Mack Gordon wrote the words to many hugely successful songs.

Words by Mack Gordon
Music by Josef Joe Myrow

20
24
mf
28
cresc.
f
32
dim.
36
mf
8vb

Stormy Weather

The 'stormy weather' in this song represents the depressed mood of the singer. The cocktail of the same name (made from rum, ginger beer and lime juice) may or may not have been named after the song!

Words by Ted Koehler
Music by Harold Arlen

mf
mf
Slowly
p
ad lib.

Night and Day

Night and Day dates from 1932, and from its very first performance has been one of Porter's best loved and most recorded songs. In 1946, an autobiographical film was made about his life, named it after this song – Cary Grant played the composer.

Words and Music by Cole Porter

25
30
f
35
39
dim.
44
rit.
f

I Got Rhythm

This song features in the 1930 musical *Girl Crazy*. In the original production it was sung by Ethel Merman, making her a Broadway star overnight. The orchestra boasted the jazz artist Benny Goodman, and the future band leader Glenn Miller.

Music and Lyrics by George Gershwin
and Ira Gershwin

mp
f
Slower
1.
Tempo I
2.

It Ain't Necessarily So

This song is from Gershwin's opera *Porgy and Bess*, considered to be his greatest musical achievement. *It Ain't Necessarily So* is filled with the rich harmonies and snappy rhythms that are typical of Gershwin's music.

Music and Lyrics by George Gershwin,
Du Bose and Dorothy Heyward and Ira Gershwin

20
25
mp
Slower
29
33
cresc.
mf
molto rit.
37

The Birth of the Blues

This song dates from 1926. The music was written by Ray Henderson, the writer of many great hits of this period, including *You're the Cream in my Coffee*. A popular Frank Sinatra recording exists of this song.

Words by Buddy De Sylva and Lew Brown
Music by Ray Henderson